DYLAN THOMAS. Before his tragic death at 39, Dylan
Thomas was already recognized as the greatest lyric poet of
the younger generation. Wide appreciation of his fiction and
other prose writings has been largely posthumous.

Born in 1914 in the Welsh seaport of Swansea, he was early
steeped in Welsh lore and poetry, and in the Bible, all of
which left their mark on his rich, startling imagery and driving
rhythms. As a boy, he said he "was small, thin, indecisively
active, quick to get dirty, curly." His formal education ended
with the Swansea Grammar school; and thereafter he was at
various times a newspaper reporter, a "hack writer," an odd-
job man, a documentary film scriptwriter.

The rich resonance of his "Welsh-singing" voice led to
Dylan Thomas reading other poets' work as well as his own
over the B.B.C. Third Programme. It also brought him to the
United States, in 1950, '52 and '53, where he gave readings
of his own and other poetry in as many as 40 university towns,
and made three magnificent long playing records published
by Caedmon. "I don't believe in New York," he said, "but I
love Third Avenue."

Since Dylan Thomas's death in 1953 his reputation and
popularity have steadily increased. His poetry is studied in
hundreds of American colleges, and his prose books such as
*Adventures in the Skin Trade, Portrait of the Artist as a
Young Dog, Quite Early One Morning* and *A Child's Christ-
mas in Wales* are paperback bestsellers. Many books have
been written about his life and work, while a play about
him, in which Alec Guinness portrayed Dylan, was a Broad-
way hit. New Directions has also published an anthology of
the poetry of other poets which Thomas recited at his
famous readings entitled *Dylan Thomas's Choice*.

UNDER MILK WOOD

Dylan Thomas

UNDER MILK WOOD

A PLAY FOR VOICES

A *New Directions* PAPERBOOK

Contents

PREFACE

On the ninth of November, 1953, a few days after his thirty-ninth birthday, Dylan Thomas died in New York. At the time of his death a new poem was still unfinished, and the collaboration with Stravinsky, planned for the end of the year, had not even begun. The survival of *Under Milk Wood* is a remarkable piece of good fortune, for it was not completed until Thomas came within a month of his death, though he had worked intermittently on the play for nearly ten years. There was no time for any final revision of the text by the poet himself, but we are justified in regarding what he has left as a complete work.

The publication of Thomas's *Collected Poems* in 1953 marked the end of one period of his literary development; after this, according to his own words, he intended to turn from the strictly personal kind of poetry to a more public form of expression, and to large-scale dramatic works, in particular, where there would be scope for all his versatility, for his gifts of humour and characterisation as well as his genius for poetry. It is fortunate that at least one of these projected works has been preserved for us.

Under Milk Wood, a Play for Voices grew by a slow and natural process, and the story of that growth, known only to a few friends of the poet, is most interesting. Thomas liked small towns by the sea best, and small Welsh towns by the sea best of all. Before the war, he lived for many years in Laugharne, and during the war, for a time in New Quay; there is no doubt that he absorbed the spirit of these places and, through imagination and insight, the spirit of all other places like them. When, more than ten years ago, a short talk was commissioned by the B.B.C., the description of a small Welsh seaside town was a natural choice of subject. *Quite Early One Morning*, short as it is, and written so many years ago, is closely related to *Under Milk Wood*. There is the same sequence of time, though limited to the morning hours and in winter, not spring; we hear the dreams of the sleeping town and see the sleepers getting up and going about their business. Captain Tiny Evans and the Reverend Thomas Evans are pygmies beside the blind seacaptain and the reverend bard of Llareggub, but Miss Hughes "The Cosy" recalls Myfanwy Price, Manchester House stands ready for Mog Edwards, and the husbands of Mrs. Ogmore-Pritchard are already at their tasks: "Dust the china, feed the canary, sweep the drawing-room floor; and before you let the sun in, mind he wipes his shoes."

The success of this broadcast talk suggested to Thomas a more extended work against the same kind of background. At first he was unable to decide upon the form of the work, and there was much discussion with friends about a stage play, a comedy in verse, and a radio play with a blind man as narrator and central character. The blind man, a natural bridge between eye and ear for the radio listener, survives in

Under Milk Wood, with the difference that Captain Cat is made to share his central position with two anonymous narrators. But the simple time sequence of *Quite Early One Morning*, which resembles the pattern of *Under Milk Wood* so closely, at first appeared inadequate; some kind of plot seemed to be necessary. Thomas thought he had found the theme he wanted in the contrast between Llareggub and the surrounding world, the conflict between the eccentrics, strong in their individuality and freedom, and the sane ones who sacrifice everything to some notion of conformity. The whole population of Llareggub cannot very well be accommodated inside the walls of a lunatic asylum; so the sane world decrees that the town itself shall be declared an "insane area," with all traffic and goods diverted from it. Captain Cat, spokesman of the indignant citizens, insists that the sanity of Llareggub should be put on trial in the townhall with every legal formality; he will be Counsel for the Defense and the citizens themselves will be witnesses. The trial takes place, but it comes to a surprising end. The final speech for the Prosecution consists of a full and minute description of the ideally sane town; as soon as they hear this, the people of Llareggub withdraw their defense and beg to be cordoned off from the sane world as soon as possible.

Once more settled in his house overlooking Laugharne Estuary, Thomas began working according to the plan of "The Town Was Mad," as he called it, and brought the action up to the delivery of letters by Willy Nilly, the postman; but by that time he had changed his mind, and there was no letter for Captain

Cat about the sanity or the insanity of the town. When this first part of *Under Milk Wood*, with the provisional title *Llareggub, a Piece for Radio Perhaps*, appeared for the first time in *Botteghe Oscure*,* Thomas had returned to the plan of *Quite Early One Morning;* his intention was to limit the picture to the town itself, with hardly a suggestion of a world beyond the town, and to extend the time sequence to form a complete cycle.

Before Thomas's third visit to the United States in 1953, the title *Under Milk Wood, a Play for Voices* was decided upon, the first part, *Llareggub*, was revised, and the work had been extended to the end of Polly Garter's Song, where it first appears. In this form, the play was read at the Kaufmann Auditorium of the Young Men's Hebrew Association on the fifteenth and the twenty-ninth of May; the poet himself read the parts of the First Voice and the Reverend Eli Jenkins.

As soon as Thomas returned to Britain, the B.B.C. urged him to complete the work without further delay, and, by omitting some projected ballads and unfinished material for the closing section, he was able to supply a finished version at the end of October. The first broadcast of the whole work, produced by Douglas Cleverdon with a distinguished all-Welsh cast, was given on January 25, 1954, with a repetition two days later.

In case *Under Milk Wood* falls into the hands of a Welsh philologist, it must be made clear that the

*Quaderno IX, edited by Marguerite Caetani (Rome, 1952).

language used is Anglo-Welsh. Dylan Thomas spoke no Welsh, and the reader must imitate his inconsistency if he wishes to hear the words as they were pronounced by the poet himself. Notes on pronunciation will be found at the end of the text.

Daniel Jones
January, 1954

A trial performance of *Under Milk Wood* was given on May 14, 1953, under the auspices of the Poetry Center of the Young Men's and Young Women's Hebrew Association, New York City. Dylan Thomas directed the production and read the parts of the First Voice, Second Drowned, Fifth Drowned, and the Reverend Eli Jenkins. The other parts were played by Dion Allen, Allen F. Collins, Roy Poole, Sada Thompson, and Nancy Wickwire.

CAST OF CHARACTERS

First Voice
Second Voice
Captain Cat
First Drowned
Second Drowned
Rosie Probert
Third Drowned
Fourth Drowned
Fifth Drowned
Mr Mog Edwards
Miss Myfanwy Price
Jack Black
Waldo's Mother
Little Boy Waldo
Waldo's Wife

Mr Waldo
First Neighbour
Second Neighbour
Third Neighbour
Fourth Neighbour
Matti's Mother
First Woman
Second Woman
Third Woman
Fourth Woman
Fifth Woman
Preacher
Mrs Ogmore-Pritchard
Mr Ogmore
Mr Pritchard

Gossamer Beynon

Organ Morgan

Utah Watkins

Mrs Utah Watkins

Ocky Milkman

A Voice

Mrs Willy Nilly

Lily Smalls

Mae Rose Cottage

Butcher Beynon

Reverend Eli Jenkins

Mr Pugh

Mrs Organ Morgan

Mary Ann Sailors

Dai Bread

Polly Garter

Nogood Boyo

Lord Cut-Glass

Voice of a Guide-Book

Mrs Beynon

Mrs Pugh

Mrs Dai Bread One

Mrs Dai Bread Two

Willy Nilly

Mrs Cherry Owen

Cherry Owen

Sinbad Sailors

Old Man

Evans the Death

Fisherman

Child's Voice

Bessie Bighead

A Drinker

UNDER MILK WOOD

UNDER MILK WOOD

[*Silence*]

FIRST VOICE (*Very softly*)

To begin at the beginning:

It is Spring, moonless night in the small town, starless and bible-black, the cobblestreets silent and the hunched, courters'-and-rabbits' wood limping invisible down to the sloeblack, slow, black, crowblack, fishingboat-bobbing sea. The houses are blind as moles (though moles see fine to-night in the snouting, velvet dingles) or blind as Captain Cat there in the muffled middle by the pump and the town clock, the shops in mourning, the Welfare Hall in widows' weeds. And all the people of the lulled and dumbfound town are sleeping now.

Hush, the babies are sleeping, the farmers, the fishers, the tradesmen and pensioners, cobbler, schoolteacher, postman and publican, the undertaker and the fancy woman, drunkard, dressmaker, preacher, policeman, the webfoot cocklewomen and the tidy wives. Young girls lie bedded soft or glide in their dreams, with rings and trousseaux, bridesmaided by glowworms down the aisles of the organplaying wood. The boys are dreaming wicked or of the bucking

1

ranches of the night and the jollyrodgered sea. And the anthracite statues of the horses sleep in the fields, and the cows in the byres, and the dogs in the wet-nosed yards; and the cats nap in the slant corners or lope sly, streaking and needling, on the one cloud of the roofs.

You can hear the dew falling, and the hushed town breathing.

Only *your* eyes are unclosed to see the black and folded town fast, and slow, asleep.

And you alone can hear the invisible starfall, the darkest-before-dawn minutely dewgrazed stir of the black, dab-filled sea where the *Arethusa*, the *Curlew* and the *Skylark, Zanzibar, Rhiannon*, the *Rover*, the *Cormorant*, and the *Star of Wales* tilt and ride.

Listen. It is night moving in the streets, the processional salt slow musical wind in Coronation Street and Cockle Row, it is the grass growing on Llareggub Hill, dewfall, starfall, the sleep of birds in Milk Wood.

Listen. It is night in the chill, squat chapel, hymning in bonnet and brooch and bombazine black, butterfly choker and bootlace bow, coughing like nanny-goats, sucking mintoes, fortywinking hallelujah; night in the four-ale, quiet as a domino; in Ocky Milkman's lofts like a mouse with gloves; in Dai Bread's bakery flying like black flour. It is to-night in Donkey Street, trotting silent, with seaweed on its hooves, along the cockled cobbles, past curtained fernpot, text and trinket, harmonium, holy dresser, watercolours done by hand, china dog and rosy tin teacaddy. It is night neddying among the snuggeries of babies.

Look. It is night, dumbly, royally winding through

the Coronation cherry trees; going through the grave-yard of Bethesda with winds gloved and folded, and dew doffed; tumbling by the Sailors Arms.

Time passes. Listen. Time passes.

Come closer now.

Only you can hear the houses sleeping in the streets in the slow deep salt and silent black, bandaged night. Only you can see, in the blinded bedrooms, the combs and petticoats over the chairs, the jugs and basins, the glasses of teeth, Thou Shalt Not on the wall, and the yellowing dickybird-watching pictures of the dead. Only you can hear and see, behind the eyes of the sleepers, the movements and countries and mazes and colours and dismays and rainbows and tunes and wishes and flight and fall and despairs and big seas of their dreams.

From where you are, you can hear their dreams.

Captain Cat, the retired blind seacaptain, asleep in his bunk in the seashelled, ship-in-bottled, shipshape best cabin of Schooner House dreams of

SECOND VOICE

never such seas as any that swamped the decks of his S.S. *Kidwelly* bellying over the bedclothes and jellyfish-slippery sucking him down salt deep into the Davy dark where the fish come biting out and nibble him down to his wishbone, and the long drowned nuzzle up to him.

FIRST DROWNED

Remember me, Captain?

3

CAPTAIN CAT
You're Dancing Williams!

FIRST DROWNED
I lost my step in Nantucket.

SECOND DROWNED
Do you see me, Captain? the white bone talking? I'm Tom-Fred the donkeyman . . . we shared the same girl once . . . her name was Mrs Probert . . .

WOMAN'S VOICE
Rosie Probert, thirty three Duck Lane. Come on up, boys, I'm dead.

THIRD DROWNED
Hold me, Captain, I'm Jonah Jarvis, come to a bad end, very enjoyable.

FOURTH DROWNED
Alfred Pomeroy Jones, sealawyer, born in Mumbles, sung like a linnet, crowned you with a flagon, tattooed with mermaids, thirst like a dredger, died of blisters.

FIRST DROWNED
This skull at your earhole is

FIFTH DROWNED
Curly Bevan. Tell my auntie it was me that pawned the ormolu clock.

CAPTAIN CAT

Aye, aye, Curly.

SECOND DROWNED

Tell my missus no I never

THIRD DROWNED

I never done what she said I never

FOURTH DROWNED

Yes, they did.

FIFTH DROWNED

And who brings coconuts and shawls and parrots
to *my* Gwen now?

FIRST DROWNED

How's it above?

SECOND DROWNED

Is there rum and lavabread?

THIRD DROWNED

Bosoms and robins?

FOURTH DROWNED

Concertinas?

FIFTH DROWNED

Ebenezer's bell?

FIRST DROWNED

Fighting and onions?

SECOND DROWNED
And sparrows and daisies?

THIRD DROWNED
Tiddlers in a jamjar?

FOURTH DROWNED
Buttermilk and whippets?

FIFTH DROWNED
Rock-a-bye baby?

FIRST DROWNED
Washing on the line?

SECOND DROWNED
And old girls in the snug?

THIRD DROWNED
How's the tenors in Dowlais?

FOURTH DROWNED
Who milks the cows in Maesgwyn?

FIFTH DROWNED
When she smiles, is there dimples?

FIRST DROWNED
What's the smell of parsley?

CAPTAIN CAT
Oh, my dead dears!

From where you are, you can hear in Cockle Row in the spring, moonless night, Miss Price, dressmaker and sweetshop-keeper, dream of

SECOND VOICE
her lover, tall as the town clock tower, Samson-syrup-gold-maned, whacking thighed and piping hot, thunderbolt-bass'd and barnacle-breasted, flailing up the cockles with his eyes like blowlamps and scooping low over her lonely loving hotwaterbottled body.

MR EDWARDS
Myfanwy Price!

MISS PRICE
Mr Mog Edwards!

MR EDWARDS
I am a draper mad with love. I love you more than all the flannelette and calico, candlewick, dimity, crash and merino, tussore, cretonne, crépon, muslin, poplin, ticking and twill in the whole Cloth Hall of the world. I have come to take you away to my Emporium on the hill, where the change hums on wires. Throw away your little bedsocks and your Welsh wool knitted jacket, I will warm the sheets like an electric toaster, I will lie by your side like the Sunday roast.

MISS PRICE
I will knit you a wallet of forget-me-not blue, for the money to be comfy. I will warm your heart by the

7

fire so that you can slip it in under your vest when the shop is closed.

Myfanwy, Myfanwy, before the mice gnaw at your bottom drawer will you say

MISS PRICE
Yes, Mog, yes, Mog, yes, yes, yes.

MR EDWARDS
And all the bells of the tills of the town shall ring for our wedding.
                    [*Noise of money-tills and chapel bells*

FIRST VOICE
Come now, drift up the dark, come up the drifting sea-dark street now in the dark night seesawing like the sea, to the bible-black airless attic over Jack Black the cobbler's shop where alone and savagely Jack Black sleeps in a nightshirt tied to his ankles with elastic and dreams of

SECOND VOICE
chasing the naughty couples down the grassgreen gooseberried double bed of the wood, flogging the tosspots in the spit-and-sawdust, driving out the bare bold girls from the sixpenny hops of his nightmares.

JACK BLACK (*Loudly*)
Ach y fi!
Ach y fi!

Evans the Death, the undertaker,

laughs high and aloud in his sleep and curls up his toes as he sees, upon waking fifty years ago, snow lie deep on the goosefield behind the sleeping house; and he runs out into the field where his mother is making welshcakes in the snow, and steals a fistful of snow-flakes and currants and climbs back to bed to eat them cold and sweet under the warm, white clothes while his mother dances in the snow kitchen crying out for her lost currants.

And in the little pink-eyed cottage next to the undertaker's, lie, alone, the seventeen snoring gentle stone of Mister Waldo, rabbitcatcher, barber, herbalist, catdoctor, quack, his fat pink hands, palms up, over the edge of the patchwork quilt, his black boots neat and tidy in the washing-basin, his bowler on a nail above the bed, a milk stout and a slice of cold bread pudding under the pillow; and, dripping in the dark, he dreams of

This little piggy went to market
This little piggy stayed at home
This little piggy had roast beef
This little piggy had none
And this little piggy went

9

LITTLE BOY
wee wee wee wee wee

MOTHER
all the way home to

WIFE (*Screaming*)
Waldo! Wal-do!

MR WALDO
Yes, Blodwen love?

WIFE
Oh, what'll the neighbours say, what'll the neighbours . . .

FIRST NEIGHBOUR
Poor Mrs Waldo

SECOND NEIGHBOUR
What she puts up with

FIRST NEIGHBOUR
Never should of married

SECOND NEIGHBOUR
If she didn't had to

FIRST NEIGHBOUR
Same as her mother

SECOND NEIGHBOUR
There's a husband for you

10

FIRST NEIGHBOUR
Bad as his father

SECOND NEIGHBOUR
And you know where he ended

FIRST NEIGHBOUR
Up in the asylum

SECOND NEIGHBOUR
Crying for his ma

FIRST NEIGHBOUR
Every Saturday

SECOND NEIGHBOUR
He hasn't got a leg

FIRST NEIGHBOUR
And carrying on

SECOND NEIGHBOUR
With that Mrs Beattie Morris

FIRST NEIGHBOUR
Up in the quarry

SECOND NEIGHBOUR
And seen her baby

FIRST NEIGHBOUR
It's got his nose

SECOND NEIGHBOUR

Oh, it makes my heart bleed

FIRST NEIGHBOUR

What he'll do for drink

SECOND NEIGHBOUR

He sold the pianola

FIRST NEIGHBOUR

And her sewing machine

SECOND NEIGHBOUR

Falling in the gutter

FIRST NEIGHBOUR

Talking to the lamp-post

SECOND NEIGHBOUR

Using language

FIRST NEIGHBOUR

Singing in the w.

SECOND NEIGHBOUR

Poor Mrs Waldo

WIFE (*Tearfully*)

... Oh, Waldo, Waldo!

MR WALDO

Hush, love, hush. I'm *widower* Waldo now.

MOTHER (*Screaming*)
Waldo, Wal-do!

LITTLE BOY
Yes, our mum?

MOTHER
Oh, what'll the neighbours say, what'll the neighbours . . .

THIRD NEIGHBOUR
Black as a chimbley

FOURTH NEIGHBOUR
Ringing doorbells

THIRD NEIGHBOUR
Breaking windows

FOURTH NEIGHBOUR
Making mudpies

THIRD NEIGHBOUR
Stealing currants

FOURTH NEIGHBOUR
Chalking words

THIRD NEIGHBOUR
Saw him in the bushes

FOURTH NEIGHBOUR
Playing mwchins

13

THIRD NEIGHBOUR

Send him to bed without any supper

FOURTH NEIGHBOUR

Give him sennapods and lock him in the dark

THIRD NEIGHBOUR

Off to the reformatory

FOURTH NEIGHBOUR

Off to the reformatory

TOGETHER

Learn him with a slipper on his b.t.m.

ANOTHER MOTHER (*Screaming*)

Waldo, Wal-do! What you doing with our Matti?

LITTLE BOY

Give us a kiss, Matti Richards.

LITTLE GIRL

Give us a penny then.

MR WALDO

I only got a halfpenny.

FIRST WOMAN

Lips is a penny.

PREACHER

Will you take this woman Matti Richards

14

SECOND WOMAN

Dulcie Prothero

THIRD WOMAN

Effie Bevan

FOURTH WOMAN

Lil the Gluepot

FIFTH WOMAN

Mrs Flusher

WIFE

Blodwen Bowen

PREACHER

To be your awful wedded wife

LITTLE BOY (*Screaming*)

No, no, no!

FIRST VOICE

Now, in her iceberg-white, holily laundered crinoline nightgown, under virtuous polar sheets, in her spruced and scoured dust-defying bedroom in trig and trim Bay View, a house for paying guests at the top of the town, Mrs Ogmore-Pritchard, widow, twice, of Mr Ogmore, linoleum, retired, and Mr Pritchard, failed bookmaker, who maddened by besoming, swabbing and scrubbing, the voice of the vacuum-cleaner and the fume of polish, ironically swallowed disinfectant, fidgets in her rinsed sleep, wakes in a dream, and nudges in the ribs dead Mr Ogmore, dead Mr Pritchard, ghostly on either side.

MRS OGMORE-PRITCHARD

Mr Ogmore!
Mr Pritchard!
It is time to inhale your balsam.

MR OGMORE

Oh, Mrs Ogmore!

MR PRITCHARD

Oh, Mrs Pritchard!

MRS PRITCHARD

Soon it will be time to get up.
Tell me your tasks, in order.

MR OGMORE

I must put my pyjamas in the drawer marked pyjamas.

MR PRITCHARD

I must take my cold bath which is good for me.

MR OGMORE

I must wear my flannel band to ward off sciatica.

MR PRITCHARD

I must dress behind the curtain and put on my apron.

MR OGMORE

I must blow my nose.

MRS OGMORE-PRITCHARD

In the garden, if you please.

MR OGMORE

In a piece of tissue-paper which I afterwards burn.

MR PRITCHARD

I must take my salts which are nature's friend.

MR OGMORE

I must boil the drinking water because of germs.

MR PRITCHARD

I must take my herb tea which is free from tannin.

MR OGMORE

And have a charcoal biscuit which is good for me.

MR PRITCHARD

I may smoke one pipe of asthma mixture.

MRS OGMORE-PRITCHARD

In the woodshed, if you please.

MR PRITCHARD

And dust the parlour and spray the canary.

MR OGMORE

I must put on rubber gloves and search the peke for fleas.

17

MR PRITCHARD
I must dust the blinds and then I must raise them.

MRS OGMORE-PRITCHARD
And before you let the sun in, mind it wipes its shoes.

FIRST VOICE
In Butcher Beynon's, Gossamer Beynon, daughter, schoolteacher, dreaming deep, daintily ferrets under a fluttering hummock of chicken's feathers in a slaughter-house that has chintz curtains and a three-pieced suite, and finds, with no surprise, a small rough ready man with a bushy tail winking in a paper carrier.

GOSSAMER BEYNON
At last, my love,

FIRST VOICE
sighs Gossamer Beynon. And the bushy tail wags rude and ginger.

ORGAN MORGAN
Help,

SECOND VOICE
cries Organ Morgan, the organist, in his dream,

ORGAN MORGAN
there is perturbation and music in Coronation Street! All the spouses are honking like geese and the babies singing opera. P.C. Attila Rees has got his

truncheon out and is playing cadenzas by the pump, the cows from Sunday Meadow ring like reindeer, and on the roof of Handel Villa see the Women's Welfare hoofing, bloomered, in the moon.

FIRST VOICE

At the sea-end of town, Mr and Mrs Floyd, the cocklers, are sleeping as quiet as death, side by wrinkled side, toothless, salt and brown, like two old kippers in a box.

And high above, in Salt Lake Farm, Mr Utah Watkins counts, all night, the wife-faced sheep as they leap the fences on the hill, smiling and knitting and bleating just like Mrs Utah Watkins.

UTAH WATKINS (*Yawning*)

Thirty-four, thirty-five, thirty-six, forty-eight, eighty-nine . . .

MRS UTAH WATKINS (*Bleating*)
Knit one slip one
Knit two together
Pass the slipstitch over . . .

FIRST VOICE

Ocky Milkman, drowned asleep in Cockle Street, is emptying his churns into the Dewi River,

OCKY MILKMAN (*Whispering*)
regardless of expense,

FIRST VOICE

and weeping like a funeral.

19

SECOND VOICE

Cherry Owen, next door, lifts a tankard to his lips but nothing flows out of it. He shakes the tankard. It turns into a fish. He drinks the fish.

FIRST VOICE

P.C. Attila Rees lumps out of bed, dead to the dark and still foghorning, and drags out his helmet from under the bed; but deep in the backyard lock-up of his sleep a mean voice murmurs

A VOICE (*Murmuring*)

You'll be sorry for this in the morning,

FIRST VOICE

and he heave-ho's back to bed. His helmet swashes in the dark.

SECOND VOICE

Willy Nilly, postman, asleep up street, walks fourteen miles to deliver the post as he does every day of the night, and rat-a-tats hard and sharp on Mrs Willy Nilly.

MRS WILLY NILLY

Don't spank me, please, teacher,

SECOND VOICE

whimpers his wife at his side, but every night of her married life she has been late for school.

Sinbad Sailors, over the taproom of the Sailors Arms, hugs his damp pillow whose secret name is Gossamer Beynon.

A mogul catches Lily Smalls in the wash-house.

LILY SMALLS

Ooh, you old mogul!

SECOND VOICE

Mrs Rose Cottage's eldest, Mae, peals off her pink-and-white skin in a furnace in a tower in a cave in a waterfall in a wood and waits there raw as an onion for Mister Right to leap up the burning tall hollow splashes of leaves like a brilliantined trout.

MAE ROSE COTTAGE (*Very close and softly, drawing out the words*)
Call me Dolores
Like they do in the stories.

FIRST VOICE

Alone until she dies, Bessie Bighead, hired help, born in the workhouse, smelling of the cowshed, snores bass and gruff on a couch of straw in a loft in Salt Lake Farm and picks a posy of daisies in Sunday Meadow to put on the grave of Gomer Owen who kissed her once by the pig-sty when she wasn't looking and never kissed her again although she was looking all the time.

And the Inspectors of Cruelty fly down into Mrs

21

Butcher Beynon's dream to persecute Mr Beynon for selling

BUTCHER BEYNON
owl meat, dogs' eyes, manchop.

SECOND VOICE
Mr Beynon, in butcher's bloodied apron, spring-heels down Coronation Street, a finger, not his own, in his mouth. Straightfaced in his cunning sleep he pulls the legs of his dreams and

BUTCHER BEYNON
hunting on pigback shoots down the wild giblets.

ORGAN MORGAN (*High and softly*)
Help!

GOSSAMER BEYNON (*Softly*)
My foxy darling.

FIRST VOICE
Now behind the eyes and secrets of the dreamers in the streets rocked to sleep by the sea, see the

SECOND VOICE
titbits and topsyturvies, bobs and buttontops, bags and bones, ash and rind and dandruff and nailparings, saliva and snowflakes and moulted feathers of dreams, the wrecks and sprats and shells and fishbones, whale-juice and moonshine and small salt fry dished up by the hidden sea.

The owls are hunting. Look, over Bethesda grave-
stones one hoots and swoops and catches a mouse by
Hannah Rees, Beloved Wife. And in Coronation
Street, which you alone can see it is so dark under the
chapel in the skies, the Reverend Eli Jenkins, poet,
preacher, turns in his deep towards-dawn sleep and
dreams of

REVEREND ELI JENKINS
Eisteddfodau.

SECOND VOICE
He intricately rhymes, to the music of crwth and
pibgorn, all night long in his druid's seedy nightie in a
beer-tent black with parchs.

FIRST VOICE
Mr Pugh, schoolmaster, fathoms asleep, pretends
to be sleeping, spies foxy round the droop of his night-
cap and pssst! whistles up

MR PUGH
Murder.

FIRST VOICE
Mrs Organ Morgan, groceress, coiled grey like a
dormouse, her paws to her ears, conjures

MRS ORGAN MORGAN
Silence.

23

SECOND VOICE

She sleeps very dulcet in a cove of wool, and trumpeting Organ Morgan at her side snores no louder than a spider.

FIRST VOICE

Mary Ann Sailors dreams of

MARY ANN SAILORS

the Garden of Eden.

FIRST VOICE

She comes in her smock-frock and clogs

MARY ANN SAILORS

away from the cool scrubbed cobbled kitchen with the Sunday-school pictures on the whitewashed wall and the farmers' almanac hung above the settle and the sides of bacon on the ceiling hooks, and goes down the cockleshelled paths of that applepie kitchen garden, ducking under the gippo's clothespegs, catching her apron on the blackcurrant bushes, past bean-rows and onion-bed and tomatoes ripening on the wall towards the old man playing the harmonium in the orchard, and sits down on the grass at his side and shells the green peas that grow up through the lap of her frock that brushes the dew.

FIRST VOICE

In Donkey Street, so furred with sleep, Dai Bread, Polly Garter, Nogood Boyo, and Lord Cut-Glass sigh before the dawn that is about to be and dream of

DAI BREAD

Harems.

POLLY GARTER

Babies.

NOGOOD BOYO

Nothing.

LORD CUT-GLASS

Tick tock tick tock tick tock tick tock.

FIRST VOICE

Time passes. Listen. Time passes. An owl flies home past Bethesda, to a chapel in an oak. And the dawn inches up.

[*One distant bell-note, faintly reverberating*

FIRST VOICE

Stand on this hill. This is Llareggub Hill, old as the hills, high, cool, and green, and from this small circle of stones, made not by druids but by Mrs Beynon's Billy, you can see all the town below you sleeping in the first of the dawn.

You can hear the love-sick woodpigeons mooning in bed. A dog barks in his sleep, farmyards away. The town ripples like a lake in the waking haze.

VOICE OF A GUIDE-BOOK

Less than five hundred souls inhabit the three quaint streets and the few narrow by-lanes and scattered farmsteads that constitute this small, decaying watering-place which may, indeed, be called a 'backwater of life' without disrespect to its natives who possess, to this day, a salty individuality of their own. The main street, Coronation Street, consists, for the most part, of humble, two-storied houses many of which attempt to achieve some measure of gaiety by prinking themselves out in crude colours and by the liberal use of pinkwash, though there are remaining a few eighteenth-century houses of more pretension, if, on the whole, in a sad state of disrepair. Though there is little to attract the hillclimber, the healthseeker, the sportsman, or the weekending motorist, the contemplative may, if sufficiently attracted to spare it some leisurely hours, find, in its cobbled streets and its little fishing harbour, in its several curious customs, and in the conversation of its local 'characters,' some of that picturesque sense of the past so frequently lacking in towns and villages which have kept more abreast of the times. The River Dewi is said to abound in trout, but is much poached. The one place of worship, with its neglected graveyard, is of no architectural interest.

[*A cock crows*

FIRST VOICE

The principality of the sky lightens now, over our green hill, into spring morning larked and crowed and belling.

[*Slow bell notes*

FIRST VOICE

Who pulls the townhall bellrope but blind Captain Cat? One by one, the sleepers are rung out of sleep this one morning as every morning. And soon you

26

shall see the chimneys' slow upflying snow as Captain Cat, in sailor's cap and seaboots, announces to-day with his loud get-out-of-bed bell.

SECOND VOICE

The Reverend Eli Jenkins, in Bethesda House, gropes out of bed into his preacher's black, combs back his bard's white hair, forgets to wash, pads barefoot downstairs, opens the front door, stands in the doorway and, looking out at the day and up at the eternal hill, and hearing the sea break and the gab of birds, remembers his own verses and tells them softly to empty Coronation Street that is rising and raising its blinds.

REVEREND ELI JENKINS

Dear Gwalia! I know there are
Towns lovelier than ours,
And fairer hills and loftier far,
And groves more full of flowers,

And boskier woods more blithe with spring
And bright with birds' adorning,
And sweeter bards than I to sing
Their praise this beauteous morning.

By Cader Idris, tempest-torn,
Or Moel yr Wyddfa's glory,
Carnedd Llewelyn beauty born,
Plinlimmon old in story,

By mountains where King Arthur dreams,
By Penmaenmawr defiant,

Llareggub Hill a molehill seems,
A pygmy to a giant.

By Sawddwy, Senny, Dovey, Dee,
Edw, Eden, Aled, all,
Taff and Towy broad and free,
Llyfnant with its waterfall,

Claerwen, Cleddau, Dulais, Daw,
Ely, Gwili, Ogwr, Nedd,
Small is our River Dewi, Lord,
A baby on a rushy bed.

By Carreg Cennen, King of time,
Our Heron Head is only
A bit of stone with seaweed spread
Where gulls come to be lonely.

A tiny dingle is Milk Wood
By Golden Grove 'neath Grongar,
But let me choose and oh! I should
Love all my life and longer

To stroll among our trees and stray
In Goosegog Lane, on Donkey Down,
And hear the Dewi sing all day,
And never, never leave the town.

SECOND VOICE
The Reverend Jenkins closes the front door. His
morning service is over.

[*Slow bell notes*

28

Now, woken at last by the out-of-bed-sleepy-head-Polly-put-the-kettle-on townhall bell, Lily Smalls, Mrs Beynon's treasure, comes downstairs from a dream of royalty who all night long went larking with her full of sauce in the Milk Wood dark, and puts the kettle on the primus ring in Mrs Beynon's kitchen, and looks at herself in Mr Beynon's shaving-glass over the sink, and sees:

LILY SMALLS

Oh there's a face!
Where you get that hair from?
Got it from a old tom cat.
Give it back then, love.
Oh, there's a perm!

Where you get that nose from, Lily?
Got it from my father, silly.
You've got it on upside down!
Oh, there's a conk!

Look at your complexion!
Oh, no, *you* look.
Needs a bit of make-up.
Needs a veil.
Oh, there's glamour!

Where you get that smile, Lil?
Never you mind, girl.
Nobody loves you.
That's what *you* think.

29

Who is it loves you?
Shan't tell.
Come on, Lily.
Cross your heart, then?
Cross my heart.

FIRST VOICE

And very softly, her lips almost touching her reflection, she breathes the name and clouds the shaving-glass.

MRS BEYNON (*Loudly, from above*)
Lily!

LILY SMALLS (*Loudly*)
Yes, mum.

MRS BEYNON
Where's my tea, girl?

LILY SMALLS
(*Softly*) Where d'you think? In the cat-box?
(*Loudly*) Coming up, mum.

FIRST VOICE

Mr Pugh, in the School House opposite, takes up the morning tea to Mrs Pugh, and whispers on the stairs

MR PUGH
Here's your arsenic, dear.
And your weedkiller biscuit.

I've throttled your parakeet.
I've spat in the vases.
I've put cheese in the mouseholes.
Here's your . . .   [*Door creaks open*
        . . . nice tea, dear.

MRS PUGH
Too much sugar.

MR PUGH
You haven't tasted it yet, dear.

MRS PUGH
Too much milk, then. Has Mr Jenkins said his
poetry?

MR PUGH
Yes, dear.

MRS PUGH
Then it's time to get up. Give me my glasses.
No, not my *reading* glasses, I want to look *out*.
I want to see

SECOND VOICE
Lily Smalls the treasure down on her red knees
washing the front step.

MRS PUGH
She's tucked her dress in her bloomers—oh, the
baggage!

P.C. Attila Rees, ox-broad, barge-booted, stamping out of Handcuff House in a heavy beef-red huff, black-browed under his damp helmet . . .

MRS PUGH

He's going to arrest Polly Garter, mark my words.

MR PUGH

What for, dear?

MRS PUGH

For having babies.

SECOND VOICE

. . . and lumbering down towards the strand to see that the sea is still there.

FIRST VOICE

Mary Ann Sailors, opening her bedroom window above the taproom and calling out to the heavens

MARY ANN SAILORS

I'm eighty-five years three months and a day!

MRS PUGH

I will say this for her, she never makes a mistake.

FIRST VOICE

Organ Morgan at his bedroom window playing chords on the sill to the morning fishwife gulls who, heckling over Donkey Street, observe

DAI BREAD

Me, Dai Bread, hurrying to the bakery, pushing in my shirt-tails, buttoning my waistcoat, ping goes a button, why can't they sew them, no time for breakfast, nothing for breakfast, there's wives for you.

MRS DAI BREAD ONE

Me, Mrs Dai Bread One, capped and shawled and no old corset, nice to be comfy, nice to be nice, clogging on the cobbles to stir up a neighbour. Oh, Mrs Sarah, can you spare a loaf, love? Dai Bread forgot the bread. There's a lovely morning! How's your boils this morning? Isn't that good news now, it's a change to sit down. Ta, Mrs Sarah.

MRS DAI BREAD TWO

Me, Mrs Dai Bread Two, gypsied to kill in a silky scarlet petticoat above my knees, dirty pretty knees, see my body through my petticoat brown as a berry, high-heel shoes with one heel missing, tortoiseshell comb in my bright black slinky hair, nothing else at all but a dab of scent, lolling gaudy at the doorway, tell your fortune in the tea-leaves, scowling at the sunshine, lighting up my pipe.

LORD CUT-GLASS

Me, Lord Cut-Glass, in an old frock-coat belonged to Eli Jenkins and a pair of postman's trousers from Bethesda Jumble, running out of doors to empty slops—mind there, Rover!—and then running in again, tick tock.

BOYO

Me, Nogood Boyo, up to no good in the wash-house.

MISS PRICE

Me, Miss Price, in my pretty print housecoat, deft at the clothesline, natty as a jenny-wren, then pit-pat back to my egg in its cosy, my crisp toast-fingers, my home-made plum and butterpat.

POLLY GARTER

Me, Polly Garter, under the washing line, giving the breast in the garden to my bonny new baby. Nothing grows in our garden, only washing. And babies. And where's their fathers live, my love? Over the hills and far away. You're looking up at me now. I know what you're thinking, you poor little milky creature. You're thinking, you're no better than you should be, Polly, and that's good enough for me. Oh, isn't life a terrible thing, thank God?

[*Single long high chord on strings*

FIRST VOICE

Now frying-pans spit, kettles and cats purr in the kitchen. The town smells of seaweed and breakfast all the way down from Bay View, where Mrs Ogmore-Pritchard, in smock and turban, big-besomed to engage the dust, picks at her starchless bread and sips lemon-rind tea, to Bottom Cottage, where Mr Waldo, in bowler and bib, gobbles his bubble-and-squeak and kippers and swigs from the saucebottle. Mary Ann Sailors

34

MARY ANN SAILORS

praises the Lord who made porridge.

FIRST VOICE

Mr Pugh

MR PUGH

remembers ground glass as he juggles his omelet.

FIRST VOICE

Mrs Pugh

MRS PUGH

nags the salt-cellar.

FIRST VOICE

Willy Nilly postman

WILLY NILLY

downs his last bucket of black brackish tea and
rumbles out bandy to the clucking back where the
hens twitch and grieve for their tea-soaked sops.

FIRST VOICE

Mrs Willy Nilly

MRS WILLY NILLY

full of tea to her double-chinned brim broods
and bubbles over her coven of kettles on the hissing
hot range always ready to steam open the mail.

FIRST VOICE

The Reverend Eli Jenkins

REVEREND ELI JENKINS
finds a rhyme and dips his pen in his cocoa.

FIRST VOICE
Lord Cut-Glass in his ticking kitchen

LORD CUT-GLASS
scampers from clock to clock, a bunch of clock-keys in one hand, a fish-head in the other.

FIRST VOICE
Captain Cat in his galley.

CAPTAIN CAT
blind and fine-fingered savours his sea-fry.

FIRST VOICE
Mr and Mrs Cherry Owen, in their Donkey Street room that is bedroom, parlour, kitchen, and scullery, sit down to last night's supper of onions boiled in their overcoats and broth of spuds and baconrind and leeks and bones.

MRS CHERRY OWEN
See that smudge on the wall by the picture of Auntie Blossom? That's where you threw the sago.
[*Cherry Owen laughs with delight*

MRS CHERRY OWEN
You only missed me by a inch.

CHERRY OWEN
I always miss Auntie Blossom too.

MRS CHERRY OWEN

Remember last night? In you reeled, my boy, as drunk as a deacon with a big wet bucket and a fish-frail full of stout and you looked at me and you said, 'God has come home!' you said, and then over the bucket you went, sprawling and bawling, and the floor was all flagons and eels.

CHERRY OWEN

Was I wounded?

MRS CHERRY OWEN

And then you took off your trousers and you said, 'Does anybody want a fight!' Oh, you old baboon.

CHERRY OWEN

Give me a kiss.

MRS CHERRY OWEN

And then you sang 'Bread of Heaven,' tenor and bass.

CHERRY OWEN

I *always* sing 'Bread of Heaven.'

MRS CHERRY OWEN

And then you did a little dance on the table.

CHERRY OWEN

I did?

MRS CHERRY OWEN

Drop dead!

CHERRY OWEN

And then what did I do?

MRS CHERRY OWEN

Then you cried like a baby and said you were a poor drunk orphan with nowhere to go but the grave.

CHERRY OWEN

And what did I do next, my dear?

MRS CHERRY OWEN

Then you danced on the table all over again and said you were King Solomon Owen and I was your Mrs Sheba.

CHERRY OWEN (*Softly*)

And then?

MRS CHERRY OWEN

And then I got you into bed and you snored all night like a brewery.

[*Mr and Mrs Cherry Owen laugh delightedly together*

FIRST VOICE

From Beynon Butchers in Coronation Street, the smell of fried liver sidles out with onions on its breath. And listen! In the dark breakfast-room behind the shop, Mr and Mrs Beynon, waited upon by their treasure, enjoy, between bites, their everymorning hullabaloo, and Mrs Beynon slips the gristly bits **under** the tasselled tablecloth to her fat cat.

[*Cat purrs*

MRS BEYNON
She likes the liver, Ben.

MR BEYNON
She ought to do, Bess. It's her brother's.

MRS BEYNON (*Screaming*)
Oh, d'you hear that, Lily?

LILY SMALLS
Yes, mum.

MRS BEYNON
We're eating pusscat.

LILY SMALLS
Yes, mum.

MRS BEYNON
Oh, you cat-butcher!

MR BEYNON
It was doctored, mind.

MRS BEYNON (*Hysterical*)
What's that got to do with it?

MR BEYNON
Yesterday we had mole.

39

MRS BEYNON

Oh, Lily, Lily!

MR BEYNON

Monday, otter. Tuesday, shrews.

                    [*Mrs Beynon screams*

LILY SMALLS

Go on, Mrs Beynon. He's the biggest liar in town.

MRS BEYNON

Don't you dare say that about Mr Beynon.

LILY SMALLS

Everybody knows it, mum.

MRS BEYNON

Mr Beynon never tells a lie. Do you, Ben?

MR BEYNON

No, Bess. And now I am going out after the corgies, with my little cleaver.

MRS BEYNON

Oh, Lily, Lily!

FIRST VOICE

Up the street, in the Sailors Arms, Sinbad Sailors, grandson of Mary Ann Sailors, draws a pint in the sunlit bar. The ship's clock in the bar says half past eleven. Half past eleven is opening time. The hands

of the clock have stayed still at half past eleven for
fifty years. It is always opening time in the Sailors
Arms.

SINBAD

Here's to me, Sinbad.

FIRST VOICE

All over the town, babies and old men are cleaned
and put into their broken prams and wheeled on to
the sunlit cockled cobbles or out into the backyards
under the dancing underclothes, and left. A baby
cries.

OLD MAN

I want my pipe and he wants his bottle.

[*School bell rings*

FIRST VOICE

Noses are wiped, heads picked, hair combed, paws
scrubbed, ears boxed, and the children shrilled off to
school.

SECOND VOICE

Fishermen grumble to their nets. Nogood Boyo
goes out in the dinghy *Zanzibar*, ships the oars, drifts
slowly in the dab-filled bay, and, lying on his back
in the unbaled water, among crabs' legs and tangled
lines, looks up at the spring sky.

NOGOOD BOYO (*Softly, lazily*)

I don't know who's up there and I don't care.

41

FIRST VOICE

He turns his head and looks up at Llareggub Hill, and sees, among green lathered trees, the white houses of the strewn away farms, where farmboys whistle, dogs shout, cows low, but all too far away for him, or you, to hear. And in the town, the shops squeak open. Mr Edwards, in butterfly-collar and straw-hat at the doorway of Manchester House, measures with his eye the dawdlers-by for striped flannel shirts and shrouds and flowery blouses, and bellows to himself in the darkness behind his eye.

MR EDWARDS (*Whispers*)

I love Miss Price.

FIRST VOICE

Syrup is sold in the post-office. A car drives to market, full of fowls and a farmer. Milk-churns stand at Coronation Corner like short silver policemen. And, sitting at the open window of Schooner House, blind Captain Cat hears all the morning of the town.

> [*School bell in background. Children's voices. The noise of children's feet on the cobbles*

CAPTAIN CAT (*Softly, to himself*)

Maggie Richards, Ricky Rhys, Tommy Powell, our Sal, little Gerwain, Billy Swansea with the dog's voice, one of Mr Waldo's, nasty Humphrey, Jackie with the sniff ... Where's Dicky's Albie? and the boys from Ty-pant? Perhaps they got the rash again.

> [*A sudden cry among the children's voices*

CAPTAIN CAT

Somebody's hit Maggie Richards. Two to one it's Billy Swansea. Never trust a boy who barks.

> [*A burst of yelping crying*

Right again! It's Billy.

FIRST VOICE

And the children's voices cry away.

> [*Postman's rat-a-tat on door, distant*

CAPTAIN CAT (*Softly, to himself*)

That's Willy Nilly knocking at Bay View. Rat-a-tat, very soft. The knocker's got a kid glove on. Who's sent a letter to Mrs Ogmore-Pritchard?

> [*Rat-a-tat, distant again*

CAPTAIN CAT

Careful now, she swabs the front glassy. Every step's like a bar of soap. Mind your size twelveses. That old Bessie would beeswax the lawn to make the birds slip.

WILLY NILLY

Morning, Mrs Ogmore-Pritchard.

MRS OGMORE-PRITCHARD

Good morning, postman.

WILLY NILLY

Here's a letter for you with stamped and addressed envelope enclosed, all the way from Builth Wells. A gentleman wants to study birds and can he have accommodation for two weeks and a bath vegetarian.

MRS OGMORE-PRITCHARD

No.

WILLY NILLY (*Persuasively*)

You wouldn't know he was in the house, Mrs Ogmore-Pritchard. He'd be out in the mornings at the bang of dawn with his bag of breadcrumbs and his little telescope ...

MRS OGMORE-PRITCHARD

And come home at all hours covered with feathers. I don't want persons in my *nice clean* rooms breathing all over the chairs ...

WILLY NILLY

Cross my heart, he won't breathe.

MRS OGMORE-PRITCHARD

... and putting their feet on my carpets and sneezing on my china and sleeping in my sheets ...

WILLY NILLY

He only wants a *single* bed, Mrs Ogmore-Pritchard.

[*Door slams*

CAPTAIN CAT (*Softly*)

And back she goes to the kitchen to polish the potatoes.

44

Captain Cat hears Willy Nilly's feet heavy on the distant cobbles.

CAPTAIN CAT

One, two, three, four, five . . . That's Mrs Rose Cottage. What's to-day? To-day she gets the letter from her sister in Gorslas. How's the twins' teeth? He's stopping at School House.

WILLY NILLY

Morning, Mrs Pugh. Mrs Ogmore-Pritchard won't have a gentleman in from Builth Wells because he'll sleep in her sheets, Mrs Rose Cottage's sister in Gorslas's twins have got to have them out . . .

MRS PUGH

Give me the parcel.

WILLY NILLY

It's for *Mr* Pugh, Mrs Pugh.

MRS PUGH

Never you mind. What's inside it?

WILLY NILLY

A book called *Lives of the Great Poisoners*.

CAPTAIN CAT

That's Manchester House.

WILLY NILLY

Morning, Mr Edwards. Very small news. Mrs Ogmore-Pritchard won't have birds in the house, and

Mr Pugh's bought a book now on how to do in Mrs Pugh.

MR EDWARDS
Have you got a letter from *her?*

WILLY NILLY
Miss Price loves you with all her heart. Smelling of lavender to-day. She's down to the last of the elderflower wine but the quince jam's bearing up and she's knitting roses on the doilies. Last week she sold three jars of boiled sweets, pound of humbugs, half a box of jellybabies and six coloured photos of Llareggub. Yours for ever. Then twenty-one X's.

MR EDWARDS
Oh, Willy Nilly, she's a ruby! Here's my letter. Put it into her hands now.
   [*Slow feet on cobbles, quicker feet approaching*

CAPTAIN CAT
Mr Waldo hurrying to the Sailors Arms. Pint of stout with a egg in it.
                    [*Footsteps stop*
(*Softly*) There's a letter for him.

WILLY NILLY
It's another paternity summons, Mr Waldo.

FIRST VOICE
The quick footsteps hurry on along the cobbles and up three steps to the Sailors Arms.

MR WALDO (*Calling out*)
Quick, Sinbad. Pint of stout. And no egg in.

FIRST VOICE
People are moving now up and down the cobbled street.

CAPTAIN CAT
All the women are out this morning, in the sun. You can tell it's Spring. There goes Mrs Cherry, you can tell her by her trotters, off she trots new as a daisy. Who's that talking by the pump? Mrs Floyd and Boyo, talking flatfish. What can you talk about flatfish? That's Mrs Dai Bread One, waltzing up the street like a jelly, every time she shakes it's slap slap slap. Who's that? Mrs Butcher Beynon with her pet black cat, it follows her everywhere, miaow and all. There goes Mrs Twenty-Three, important, the sun gets up and goes down in her dewlap, when she shuts her eyes, it's night. High heels now, in the morning too, Mrs Rose Cottage's eldest Mae, seventeen and never been kissed ho ho, going young and milking under my window to the field with the nannygoats, she reminds me all the way. Can't hear what the women are gabbing round the pump. Same as ever. Who's having a baby, who blacked whose eye, seen Polly Garter giving her belly an airing, there should be a law, seen Mrs Beynon's new mauve jumper, it's her old grey jumper dyed, who's dead, who's dying, there's a lovely day, oh the cost of soapflakes!

[*Organ music, distant*

47

CAPTAIN CAT

Organ Morgan's at it early. You can *tell* it's Spring.

FIRST VOICE

And he hears the noise of milk-cans.

CAPTAIN CAT

Ocky Milkman on his round. I will say this, his milk's as fresh as the dew. Half dew it is. Snuffle on, Ocky, watering the town . . . Somebody's coming. Now the voices round the pump can see somebody coming. Hush, there's a hush! You can tell by the noise of the hush, it's Polly Garter. (*Louder*) Hullo, Polly, who's there?

POLLY GARTER (*Off*)

Me, love.

CAPTAIN CAT

That's Polly Garter. (*Softly*) Hullo, Polly, my love, can you hear the dumb goose-hiss of the wives as they huddle and peck or flounce at a waddle away? Who cuddled you when? Which of their gandering hubbies moaned in Milk Wood for your naughty mothering arms and body like a wardrobe, love? Scrub the floors of the Welfare Hall for the Mothers' Union Social Dance, you're one mother won't wriggle her roly poly bum or pat her fat little buttery feet in that wedding-ringed holy to-night through the waltzing breadwinners snatched from the cosy smoke of the Sailors Arms will grizzle and mope.

[*A cock crows*

CAPTAIN CAT

Too late, cock, too late

SECOND VOICE

for the town's half over with its morning. The morning's busy as bees.

[*Organ music fades into silence*

FIRST VOICE

There's the clip clop of horses on the sunhoneyed cobbles of the humming streets, hammering of horse-shoes, gobble quack and cackle, tomtit twitter from the bird-ounced boughs, braying on Donkey Down. Bread is baking, pigs are grunting, chop goes the butcher, milk-churns bell, tills ring, sheep cough, dogs shout, saws sing. Oh, the Spring whinny and morning moo from the clog-dancing farms, the gulls' gab and rabble on the boat-bobbing river and sea and the cockles bubbling in the sand, scamper of sander-lings, curlew cry, crow caw, pigeon coo, clock strike, bull bellow, and the ragged gabble of the beargarden school as the women scratch and babble in Mrs Organ Morgan's general shop where everything is sold: custard, buckets, henna, rat-traps, shrimp-nets, sugar, stamps, confetti, paraffin, hatchets, whistles.

FIRST WOMAN

Mrs Ogmore-Pritchard

SECOND WOMAN

la di da

FIRST WOMAN

got a man in Builth Wells

THIRD WOMAN

and he got a little telescope to look at birds

SECOND WOMAN

Willy Nilly said

THIRD WOMAN

Remember her first husband? He didn't need a telescope

FIRST WOMAN

he looked at them undressing through the keyhole

THIRD WOMAN

and he used to shout Tallyho

SECOND WOMAN

but Mr Ogmore was a proper gentleman

FIRST WOMAN

even though he hanged his collie.

THIRD WOMAN

Seen Mrs Butcher Beynon?

SECOND WOMAN

she said Butcher Beynon put dogs in the mincer

FIRST WOMAN

go on, he's pulling her leg

THIRD WOMAN

now don't you dare tell her that, there's a dear

SECOND WOMAN

or she'll think he's trying to pull it off and eat it.

FOURTH WOMAN

There's a nasty lot live here when you come to think.

FIRST WOMAN

Look at that Nogood Boyo now

SECOND WOMAN

too lazy to wipe his snout

THIRD WOMAN

and going out fishing every day and all he ever brought back was a Mrs Samuels

FIRST WOMAN

been in the water a week.

SECOND WOMAN

And look at Ocky Milkman's wife that nobody's ever seen

FIRST WOMAN

he keeps her in the cupboard with the empties

THIRD WOMAN

and think of Dai Bread with two wives

one for the daytime one for the night.

FOURTH WOMAN
Men are brutes on the quiet.

THIRD WOMAN
And how's Organ Morgan, Mrs Morgan?

FIRST WOMAN
you look dead beat

SECOND WOMAN
it's organ organ all the time with him

THIRD WOMAN
up every night until midnight playing the organ

MRS ORGAN MORGAN
Oh, I'm a martyr to music.

FIRST VOICE
Outside, the sun springs down on the rough and tumbling town. It runs through the hedges of Goose-gog Lane, cuffing the birds to sing. Spring whips green down Cockle Row, and the shells ring out. Llareggub this snip of a morning is wildfruit and warm, the streets, fields, sands and waters springing in the young sun.

SECOND VOICE
Evans the Death presses hard with black gloves on the coffin of his breast in case his heart jumps out.

EVANS THE DEATH (*Harshly*)
Where's your dignity. Lie down.

SECOND VOICE
Spring stirs Gossamer Beynon schoolmistress like a spoon.

GOSSAMER BEYNON (*Tearfully*)
Oh, what can I do? I'll *never* be refined if I twitch.

SECOND VOICE
Spring this strong morning foams in a flame in Jack Black as he cobbles a high-heeled shoe for Mrs Dai Bread Two the gypsy, but he hammers it sternly out.

JACK BLACK (*To a hammer rhythm*)
There is *no leg* belonging to the foot that belongs to this shoe.

SECOND VOICE
The sun and the green breeze ship Captain Cat sea-memory again.

CAPTAIN CAT
No, *I'll* take the mulatto, by God, who's captain here? Parlez-vous jig jig, Madam?

SECOND VOICE
Mary Ann Sailors says very softly to herself as she looks out at Llareggub Hill from the bedroom where she was born

53

MARY ANN SAILORS (*Loudly*)

It is Spring in Llareggub in the sun in my old age, and this is the Chosen Land.

[*A choir of children's voices suddenly cries out on one, high, glad, long, sighing note*

FIRST VOICE

And in Willy Nilly the Postman's dark and sizzling damp tea-coated misty pygmy kitchen where the spittingcat kettles throb and hop on the range, Mrs Willy Nilly steams open Mr Mog Edwards' letter to Miss Myfanwy Price and reads it aloud to Willy Nilly by the squint of the Spring sun through the one sealed window running with tears, while the drugged, bedraggled hens at the back door whimper and snivel for the lickerish bog-black tea.

MRS WILLY NILLY

From Manchester House, Llareggub. Sole Prop: Mr Mog Edwards (late of Twll), Linendraper, Haberdasher, Master Tailor, Costumier. For West End Negligee, Lingerie, Teagowns, Evening Dress, Trousseaux, Layettes. Also Ready to Wear for All Occasions. Economical Outfitting for Agricultural Employment Our Speciality, Wardrobes Bought. Among Our Satisfied Customers Ministers of Religion and J.P.'s. Fittings by Appointment. Advertising Weekly in the *Twll Bugle*. Beloved Myfanwy Price my Bride in Heaven,

MOG EDWARDS

I love you until Death do us part and then we shall be together for ever and ever. A new parcel of ribbons has come from Carmarthen to-day, all the colours in the rainbow. I wish I could tie a ribbon in your hair a white one but it cannot be. I dreamed last night you were all dripping wet and you sat on my lap as the Reverend Jenkins went down the street. I see you got a mermaid in your lap he said and he lifted his hat. He is a proper Christian. Not like Cherry Owen who said you should have thrown her back he said. Business is very poorly. Polly Garter bought two garters with roses but she never got stockings so what is the use I say. Mr Waldo tried to sell me a woman's nightie outsize he said he found it and we know where. I sold a packet of pins to Tom the Sailors to pick his teeth. If this goes on I shall be in the poorhouse. My heart is in your bosom and yours is in mine. God be with you always Myfanwy Price and keep you lovely for me in His Heavenly Mansion. I must stop now and remain, Your Eternal, Mog Edwards.

MRS WILLY NILLY

And then a little message with a rubber stamp. Shop at Mog's!!!

FIRST VOICE

And Willy Nilly, rumbling, jockeys out again to the three-seated shack called the House of Commons in the back where the hens weep, and sees, in sudden Springshine,

SECOND VOICE

herring gulls heckling down to the harbour where the fishermen spit and prop the morning up and eye the fishy sea smooth to the sea's end as it lulls in blue. Green and gold money, tobacco, tinned salmon, hats with feathers, pots of fish-paste, warmth for the winter-to-be, weave and leap in it rich and slippery in the flash and shapes of fishes through the cold sea-streets. But with blue lazy eyes the fishermen gaze at that milkmaid whispering water with no ruck or ripple as though it blew great guns and serpents and typhooned the town.

FISHERMAN

Too rough for fishing to-day.

SECOND VOICE

And they thank God, and gob at a gull for luck, and moss-slow and silent make their way uphill, from the still still sea, towards the Sailors Arms as the children

[*School bell*

FIRST VOICE

spank and scamper rough and singing out of school into the draggletail yard. And Captain Cat at his window says soft to himself the words of their song.

CAPTAIN CAT (*To the beat of the singing*)
Johnnie Crack and Flossie Snail
Kept their baby in a milking pail
Flossie Snail and Johnnie Crack
One would pull it out and one would put it back

O it's my turn now said Flossie Snail
To take the baby from the milking pail

56

And it's my turn now said Johnnie Crack
To smack it on the head and put it back

Johnnie Crack and Flossie Snail
Kept their baby in a milking pail
One would put it back and one would pull it out
And all it had to drink was ale and stout
For Johnnie Crack and Flossie Snail
Always used to say that stout and ale
Was *good* for a baby in a milking pail.

[*Long pause*

FIRST VOICE

The music of the spheres is heard distinctly over
Milk Wood. It is 'The Rustle of Spring.'

SECOND VOICE

A glee-party sings in Bethesda Graveyard, gay
but muffled.

FIRST VOICE

Vegetables make love above the tenors

SECOND VOICE

and dogs bark blue in the face.

FIRST VOICE

Mrs Ogmore-Pritchard belches in a teeny hanky
and chases the sunlight with a flywhisk, but even she
cannot drive out the Spring: from one of the finger-
bowls, a primrose grows.

SECOND VOICE

Mrs Dai Bread One and Mrs Dai Bread Two are sitting outside their house in Donkey Lane, one darkly one plumply blooming in the quick, dewy sun. Mrs Dai Bread Two is looking into a crystal ball which she holds in the lap of her dirty yellow petticoat, hard against her hard dark thighs.

MRS DAI BREAD TWO

Cross my palm with silver. Out of our housekeeping money. Aah!

MRS DAI BREAD ONE

What d'you see, lovie?

MRS DAI BREAD TWO

I see a featherbed. With three pillows on it. And a text above the bed. I can't read what it says, there's great clouds blowing. Now they have blown away. God is Love, the text says.

MRS DAI BREAD ONE (*Delighted*)

That's *our* bed.

MRS DAI BREAD TWO

And now it's vanished. The sun's spinning like a top. Who's this coming out of the sun? It's a hairy little man with big pink lips. He got a wall eye.

MRS DAI BREAD ONE

It's Dai, it's Dai Bread!

Ssh! The featherbed's floating back. The little man's taking his boots off. He's pulling his shirt over his head. He's beating his chest with his fists. He's climbing into bed.

MRS DAI BREAD ONE

Go on, go on.

MRS DAI BREAD TWO

There's *two* women in bed. He looks at them both, with his head cocked on one side. He's whistling through his teeth. Now he grips his little arms round one of the women.

MRS DAI BREAD ONE

Which one, which one?

MRS DAI BREAD TWO

I can't see any more. There's great clouds blowing again.

MRS DAI BREAD ONE

Ach, the mean old clouds!
[*Pause. The children's singing fades*

FIRST VOICE

The morning is all singing. The Reverend Eli Jenkins, busy on his morning calls, stops outside the Welfare Hall to hear Polly Garter as she scrubs the floors for the Mothers' Union Dance to-night.

POLLY GARTER (*Singing*)

I loved a man whose name was Tom
He was strong as a bear and two yards long
I loved a man whose name was Dick
He was big as a barrel and three feet thick
And I loved a man whose name was Harry
Six feet tall and sweet as a cherry
But the one I loved best awake or asleep
Was little Willy Wee and he's six feet deep.

O Tom Dick and Harry were three fine men
And I'll never have such loving again
But little Willy Wee who took me on his knee
Little Willy Wee was the man for me.

Now men from every parish round
Run after me and roll me on the ground
But whenever I love another man back
Johnnie from the Hill or Sailing Jack
I always think as they do what they please
Of Tom Dick and Harry who were tall as trees
And most I think when I'm by their side
Of little Willy Wee who downed and died.

O Tom Dick and Harry were three fine men
And I'll never have such loving again
But little Willy Wee who took me on his knee
Little Willy Weazel is the man for me.

REVEREND ELI JENKINS
Praise the Lord! We are a musical nation.

SECOND VOICE

And the Reverend Jenkins hurries on through the town to visit the sick with jelly and poems.

FIRST VOICE

The town's as full as a lovebird's egg.

MR WALDO

There goes the Reverend,

FIRST VOICE

says Mr Waldo at the smoked herring brown window of the unwashed Sailors Arms,

MR WALDO

with his brolly and his odes. Fill 'em up, Sinbad, I'm on the treacle to-day.

SECOND VOICE

The silent fishermen flush down their pints.

SINBAD

Oh, Mr Waldo,

FIRST VOICE

sighs Sinbad Sailors,

SINBAD

I dote on that Gossamer Beynon. She's a lady all over.

FIRST VOICE

And Mr Waldo, who is thinking of a woman soft as Eve and sharp as sciatica to share his bread-pudding bed, answers

MR WALDO

No lady that I know is.

SINBAD

And if only grandma'd die, cross my heart I'd go down on my knees Mr Waldo and I'd say Miss Gossamer I'd say

CHILDREN'S VOICES

When birds do sing hey ding a ding a ding
Sweet lovers love the Spring . . .

SECOND VOICE

Polly Garter sings, still on her knees,

POLLY GARTER

Tom Dick and Harry were three fine men
And I'll never have such

CHILDREN

Ding a ding

POLLY GARTER

again.

FIRST VOICE

And the morning school is over, and Captain Cat at his curtained schooner's porthole open to the Spring

sun tides hears the naughty forfeiting children tumble
and rhyme on the cobbles.

GIRLS' VOICES
Gwennie call the boys
They make such a noise.

GIRL

Boys boys boys
Come along to me.

GIRLS' VOICES
Boys boys boys
Kiss Gwennie where she says
Or give her a penny.
Go on, Gwennie.

GIRL
Kiss me in Goosegog Lane
Or give me a penny.
What's your name?

FIRST BOY
Billy.

GIRL
Kiss me in Goosegog Lane Billy
Or give me a penny silly.

FIRST BOY
Gwennie Gwennie
I kiss you in Goosegog Lane.
Now I haven't got to give you a penny.

Boys boys boys
Kiss Gwennie where she says
Or give her a penny.
Go on, Gwennie.

GIRL

Kiss me on Llareggub Hill
Or give me a penny.
What's your name?

SECOND BOY

Johnnie Cristo.

GIRL

Kiss me on Llareggub Hill Johnnie Cristo
Or give me a penny mister.

SECOND BOY

Gwennie Gwennie
I kiss you on Llareggub Hill.
Now I haven't got to give you a penny.

GIRLS' VOICES

Boys boys boys
Kiss Gwennie where she says
Or give her a penny.
Go on, Gwennie.

GIRL

Kiss me in Milk Wood
Or give me a penny.
What's your name?

Dicky.

GIRL
Kiss me in Milk Wood Dicky
Or give me a penny quickly.

THIRD BOY
Gwennie Gwennie
I can't kiss you in Milk Wood.

GIRLS' VOICES
Gwennie ask him why.

GIRL
Why?

THIRD BOY
Because my mother says I mustn't.

GIRLS' VOICES
Cowardy cowardy custard
Give Gwennie a penny.

GIRL
Give me a penny.

THIRD BOY
I haven't got any.

GIRLS' VOICES
Put him in the river
Up to his liver

Quick quick Dirty Dick
Beat him on the bum
With a rhubarb stick.
Aiee!
Hush!

And the shrill girls giggle and master around him and squeal as they clutch and thrash, and he blubbers away downhill with his patched pants falling, and his tear-splashed blush burns all the way as the triumphant bird-like sisters scream with buttons in their claws and the bully brothers hoot after him his little nick-name and his mother's shame and his father's wicked-ness with the loose wild barefoot women of the hovels of the hills. It all means nothing at all, and, howling for his milky mum, for her cawl and buttermilk and cowbreath and welshcakes and the fat birth-smelling bed and moonlit kitchen of her arms, he'll never forget as he paddles blind home through the weeping end of the world. Then his tormentors tussle and run to the Cockle Street sweet-shop, their pennies sticky as honey, to buy from Miss Myfanwy Price, who is cocky and neat as a puff-bosomed robin and her small round buttocks tight as ticks, gobstoppers big as wens that rainbow as you suck, brandyballs, winegums, hundreds and thousands, liquorice sweet as sick, nougat to tug and ribbon out like another red rubbery tongue, gum to glue in girls' curls, crimson cough-drops to spit blood, ice-cream cornets, dandelion-and-burdock, raspberry and cherryade, pop goes the weasel and the wind.

Gossamer Beynon high-heels out of school. The
sun hums down through the cotton flowers of her
dress into the bell of her heart and buzzes in the
honey there and couches and kisses, lazy-loving and
boozed, in her red-berried breast. Eyes run from the
trees and windows of the street, steaming 'Gossamer,'
and strip her to the nipples and the bees. She blazes
naked past the Sailors Arms, the only woman on
the Dai-Adamed earth. Sinbad Sailors places on her
thighs still dewdamp from the first mangrowing cock-
crow garden his reverent goat-bearded hands.

GOSSAMER BEYNON

I don't care if he *is* common,

SECOND VOICE

she whispers to her salad-day deep self,

GOSSAMER BEYNON

I want to gobble him up. I don't care if he *does*
drop his aitches,

SECOND VOICE

she tells the stripped and mother-of-the-world big-
beamed and Eve-hipped spring of her self.

GOSSAMER BEYNON

so long as he's all cucumber and hooves.

SECOND VOICE

Sinbad Sailors watches her go by, demure and
proud and schoolmarm in her crisp flower dress and

sun-defying hat, with never a look or lilt or wriggle, the butcher's unmelting icemaiden daughter veiled forever from the hungry hug of his eyes.

SINBAD SAILORS

Oh, Gossamer Beynon, why are you so proud?

SECOND VOICE

he grieves to his Guinness,

SINBAD SAILORS

Oh, beautiful beautiful Gossamer B, I wish I wish that you were for me. I wish you were not so edu-cated.

SECOND VOICE

She feels his goatbeard tickle her in the middle of the world like a tuft of wiry fire, and she turns in a terror of delight away from his whips and whiskery conflagration, and sits down in the kitchen to a plate heaped high with chips and the kidneys of lambs.

FIRST VOICE

In the blind-drawn dark dining-room of School House, dusty and echoing as a dining-room in a vault, Mr and Mrs Pugh are silent over cold grey cottage pie. Mr Pugh reads, as he forks the shroud meat in, from *Lives of the Great Poisoners.* He has bound a plain brown-paper cover round the book. Slyly, between slow mouthfuls, he sidespies up at Mrs Pugh, poisons her with his eye, then goes on reading. He under-lines certain passages and smiles in secret.

MRS PUGH

Persons with manners do not read at table,

FIRST VOICE

says Mrs Pugh. She swallows a digestive tablet as big as a horse-pill, washing it down with clouded peasoup water.

[*Pause*

MRS PUGH

Some persons were brought up in pigsties.

MR PUGH

Pigs don't read at table, dear.

FIRST VOICE

Bitterly she flicks dust from the broken cruet. It settles on the pie in a thin gnat-rain.

MR PUGH

Pigs can't read, my dear.

MRS PUGH

I know one who can.

FIRST VOICE

Alone in the hissing laboratory of his wishes, Mr Pugh minces among bad vats and jeroboams, tiptoes through spinneys of murdering herbs, agony dancing in his crucibles, and mixes especially for Mrs Pugh a venomous porridge unknown to toxicologists which will scald and viper through her until her ears fall off

69

like figs, her toes grow big and black as balloons, and steam comes screaming out of her navel.

MR PUGH

You know best, dear,

FIRST VOICE

says Mr Pugh, and quick as a flash he ducks her in rat soup.

MRS PUGH

What's that book by your trough, Mr Pugh?

MR PUGH

It's a theological work, my dear. *Lives of the Great Saints.*

FIRST VOICE

Mrs Pugh smiles. An icicle forms in the cold air of the dining vault.

MRS PUGH

I saw you talking to a saint this morning. Saint Polly Garter. She was martyred again last night. Mrs Organ Morgan saw her with Mr Waldo.

MRS ORGAN MORGAN

And when they saw me they pretended they were looking for nests,

SECOND VOICE

said Mrs Organ Morgan to her husband, with her mouth full of fish as a pelican's.

MRS ORGAN MORGAN

But you don't go nesting in long combinations, I said to myself, like Mr Waldo was wearing, and your dress nearly over your head like Polly Garter's. Oh, they didn't fool me.

SECOND VOICE

One big bird gulp, and the flounder's gone. She licks her lips and goes stabbing again.

MRS ORGAN MORGAN

And when you think of all those babies she's got, then all I can say is she'd better give up bird nesting that's all I can say, it isn't the right kind of hobby at all for a woman that can't say No even to midgets. Remember Bob Spit? He wasn't any bigger than a baby and he gave her two. But they're two nice boys, I will say that, Fred Spit and Arthur. Sometimes I like Fred best and sometimes I like Arthur. Who do you like best, Organ?

ORGAN MORGAN

Oh, Bach without any doubt. Bach every time for me.

MRS ORGAN MORGAN

Organ Morgan, you haven't been listening to a word I said. It's organ organ all the time with you...

FIRST VOICE

And she bursts into tears, and, in the middle of her salty howling, nimbly spears a small flatfish and pelicans it whole.

And then Palestrina,

says Organ Morgan.

Lord Cut-Glass, in his kitchen full of time, squats down alone to a dogdish, marked Fido, of peppery fish-scraps and listens to the voices of his sixty-six clocks—(one for each year of his loony age)—and watches, with love, their black-and-white moony loudlipped faces tocking the earth away: slow clocks, quick clocks, pendulumed heart-knocks, china, alarm, grandfather, cuckoo; clocks shaped like Noah's whirring Ark, clocks that bicker in marble ships, clocks in the wombs of glass women, hourglass chimers, tu-wit-tu-woo clocks, clocks that pluck tunes, Vesuvius clocks all black bells and lava, Niagara clocks that cataract their ticks, old time-weeping clocks with ebony beards, clocks with no hands for ever drumming out time without ever knowing what time it is. His sixty-six singers are all set at different hours. Lord Cut-Glass lives in a house and a life at siege. Any minute or dark day now, the unknown enemy will loot and savage downhill, but they will not catch him napping. Sixty-six different times in his fish-slimy kitchen ping, strike, tick, chime, and tock.

The lust and lilt and lather and emerald breeze and crackle of the bird-praise and body of Spring with

72

its breasts full of rivering May-milk, means, to that
lordly fish-head nibbler, nothing but another nearness
to the tribes and navies of the Last Black Day who'll
sear and pillage down Armageddon Hill to his double-
locked rusty-shuttered tick-tock dust-scrabbled shack
at the bottom of the town that has fallen head over
bells in love.

POLLY GARTER

And I'll never have such loving again,

SECOND VOICE

pretty Polly hums and longs.

POLLY GARTER (*Sings*)

Now when farmers' boys on the first fair day
Come down from the hills to drink and be gay,
Before the sun sinks I'll lie there in their arms
For they're *good* bad boys from the lonely farms,

But I always think as we tumble into bed
Of little Willy Wee who is dead, dead, dead . . .
                                    [*A silence*

FIRST VOICE

The sunny slow lulling afternoon yawns and
moons through the dozy town. The sea lolls, laps and
idles in, with fishes sleeping in its lap. The meadows
still as Sunday, the shut-eye tasselled bulls, the goat-
and-daisy dingles, nap happy and lazy. The dumb
duck-ponds snooze. Clouds sag and pillow on Llareg-
gub Hill. Pigs grunt in a wet wallow-bath, and smile

as they snort and dream. They dream of the acorned swill of the world, the rooting for pig-fruit, the bag-pipe dugs of the mother sow, the squeal and snuffle of yesses of the women pigs in rut. They mud-bask and snout in the pig-loving sun; their tails curl; they rollick and slobber and snore to deep, smug, after-swill sleep. Donkeys angelically drowse on Donkey Down.

MRS PUGH

Persons with manners,

SECOND VOICE

snaps Mrs cold Pugh

MRS PUGH

do not nod at table.

FIRST VOICE

Mr Pugh cringes awake. He puts on a soft-soaping smile: it is sad and grey under his nicotine-eggyellow weeping walrus Victorian moustache worn thick and long in memory of Doctor Crippen.

MRS PUGH

You should wait until you retire to your sty,

SECOND VOICE

says Mrs Pugh, sweet as a razor. His fawning measly quarter-smile freezes. Sly and silent, he foxes into his chemist's den and there, in a hiss and prussic circle of cauldrons and phials brimful with pox and

the Black Death, cooks up a fricassee of deadly night-
shade, nicotine, hot frog, cyanide and bat-spit for his
needling stalactite hag and bednag of a pokerbacked
nutcracker wife.

MR PUGH

I beg your pardon, my dear,

SECOND VOICE

he murmurs with a wheedle.

FIRST VOICE

Captain Cat, at his window thrown wide to the
sun and the clippered seas he sailed long ago when his
eyes were blue and bright, slumbers and voyages; ear-
ringed and rolling, I Love You Rosie Probert tattooed
on his belly, he brawls with broken bottles in the fug
and babel of the dark dock bars, roves with a herd of
short and good time cows in every naughty port and
twines and souses with the drowned and blowzy-
breasted dead. He weeps as he sleeps and sails.

SECOND VOICE

One voice of all he remembers most dearly as his
dream buckets down. Lazy early Rosie with the flaxen
thatch, whom he shared with Tom-Fred the donkey-
man and many another seaman, clearly and near to
him speaks from the bedroom of her dust. In that gulf
and haven, fleets by the dozen have anchored for the
little heaven of the night; but she speaks to Captain
napping Cat alone. Mrs Probert . . .

ROSIE PROBERT

from Duck Lane, Jack. Quack twice and ask for
Rosie.

SECOND VOICE

. . . is the one love of his sea-life that was sardined
with women.

ROSIE PROBERT (*Softly*)
What seas did you see,
Tom Cat, Tom Cat,
In your sailoring days
Long long ago?
What sea beasts were
In the wavery green
When you were my master?

CAPTAIN CAT
I'll tell you the truth.
Seas barking like seals,
Blue seas and green,
Seas covered with eels
And mermen and whales.

ROSIE PROBERT
What seas did you sail
Old whaler when
On the blubbery waves
Between Frisco and Wales
You were my bosun?

CAPTAIN CAT
As true as I'm here

76

Dear you Tom Cat's tart
You landlubber Rosie
You cosy love
My easy as easy
My true sweetheart,
Seas green as a bean
Seas gliding with swans
In the seal-barking moon.

ROSIE PROBERT
What seas were rocking
My little deck hand
My favourite husband
In your seaboots and hunger
My duck my whaler
My honey my daddy
My pretty sugar sailor
With my name on your belly
When you were a boy
Long long ago?

CAPTAIN CAT
I'll tell you no lies.
The only sea I saw
Was the seesaw sea
With you riding on it.
Lie down, lie easy.
Let me shipwreck in your thighs.

ROSIE PROBERT
Knock twice, Jack,

At the door of my grave
And ask for Rosie.

CAPTAIN CAT
Rosie Probert.

ROSIE PROBERT
Remember her.
She is forgetting.
The earth which filled her mouth
Is vanishing from her.
Remember me.
I have forgotten you.
I am going into the darkness of the
darkness for ever.
I have forgotten that I was ever born.

CHILD
Look,

FIRST VOICE
says a child to her mother as they pass by the
window of Schooner House,

CHILD
Captain Cat is crying.

FIRST VOICE
Captain Cat is crying

CAPTAIN CAT
Come back, come back,

FIRST VOICE
up the silences and echoes of the passages of the
eternal night.

CHILD
He's crying all over his nose,

FIRST VOICE
says the child. Mother and child move on down
the street.

CHILD
He's got a nose like strawberries,

FIRST VOICE
the child says; and then she forgets him too. She
sees in the still middle of the bluebagged bay Nogood
Boyo fishing from the *Zanzibar*.

CHILD
Nogood Boyo gave me three pennies yesterday
but I wouldn't,

FIRST VOICE
the child tells her mother.

SECOND VOICE
Boyo catches a whalebone corset. It is all he has
caught all day.

NOGOOD BOYO
Bloody funny fish!

SECOND VOICE

Mrs Dai Bread Two gypsies up his mind's slow eye, dressed only in a bangle.

NOGOOD BOYO

She's wearing her nightgown. (*Pleadingly*) Would you like this nice wet corset, Mrs Dai Bread Two?

MRS DAI BREAD TWO

No, I *won't!*

NOGOOD BOYO

And a bite of my little apple?

SECOND VOICE

he offers with no hope.

FIRST VOICE

She shakes her brass nightgown, and he chases her out of his mind; and when he comes gusting back, there in the bloodshot centre of his eye a geisha girl grins and bows in a kimono of ricepaper.

NOGOOD BOYO

I want to be *good* Boyo, but nobody'll let me,

FIRST VOICE

he sighs as she writhes politely. The land fades, the sea flocks silently away; and through the warm white cloud where he lies, silky, tingling, uneasy Eastern music undoes him in a Japanese minute.

The afternoon buzzes like lazy bees round the flowers round Mae Rose Cottage. Nearly asleep in the field of nannygoats who hum and gently butt the sun, she blows love on a puffball.

MAE ROSE COTTAGE (*Lazily*)
He loves me
He loves me not
He loves me
He loves me not
He *loves* me!—the dirty old fool.

SECOND VOICE
Lazy she lies alone in clover and sweet-grass, seventeen and never been sweet in the grass ho ho.

FIRST VOICE
The Reverend Eli Jenkins inky in his cool front parlour or poem-room tells only the truth in his Lifework—the Population, Main Industry, Shipping, History, Topography, Flora and Fauna of the town he worships in—the White Book of Llareggub. Portraits of famous bards and preachers, all fur and wool from the squint to the kneecaps, hang over him heavy as sheep, next to faint lady watercolours of pale green Milk Wood like a lettuce salad dying. His mother, propped against a pot in a palm, with her wedding-ring waist and bust like a black-clothed dining-table, suffers in her stays.

REVEREND ELI JENKINS

Oh, angels be careful there with your knives and forks,

FIRST VOICE

he prays. There is no known likeness of his father Esau, who, undogcollared because of his little weakness, was scythed to the bone one harvest by mistake when sleeping with his weakness in the corn. He lost all ambition and died, with one leg.

REVEREND ELI JENKINS

Poor Dad,

SECOND VOICE

grieves the Reverend Eli,

REVEREND ELI JENKINS

to die of drink and agriculture.

SECOND VOICE

Farmer Watkins in Salt Lake Farm hates his cattle on the hill as he ho's them in to milking.

UTAH WATKINS (*In a fury*)

Damn you, you damned dairies!

SECOND VOICE

A cow kisses him.

UTAH WATKINS

Bite her to death!

SECOND VOICE

he shouts to his deaf dog who smiles and licks his hands.

UTAH WATKINS

Gore him, sit on him, Daisy!

SECOND VOICE

he bawls to the cow who barbed him with her tongue, and she moos gentle words as he raves and dances among his summerbreathed slaves walking delicately to the farm. The coming of the end of the Spring day is already reflected in the lakes of their great eyes. Bessie Bighead greets them by the names she gave them when they were maidens.

BESSIE BIGHEAD

Peg, Meg, Buttercup, Moll,
Fan from the Castle,
Theodosia and Daisy.

SECOND VOICE

They bow their heads.

FIRST VOICE

Look up Bessie Bighead in the White Book of Llareggub and you will find the few haggard rags and the one poor glittering thread of her history laid out in pages there with as much love and care as the lock of hair of a first lost love. Conceived in Milk Wood, born in a barn, wrapped in paper, left on a doorstep, big-headed and bass-voiced she grew in the dark until long-dead Gomer Owen kissed her when she wasn't looking because he was dared. Now in the light she'll work, sing, milk, say the cows' sweet names and sleep until the night sucks out her soul and spits it into the sky. In her life-long love light, holily Bessie milks the fond lake-eyed cows as dusk showers slowly down over byre, sea and town.

Utah Watkins curses through the farmyard on a carthorse.

UTAH WATKINS
Gallop, you bleeding cripple!

FIRST VOICE
and the huge horse neighs softly as though he had given it a lump of sugar.

Now the town is dusk. Each cobble, donkey, goose and gooseberry street is a thoroughfare of dusk; and dusk and ceremonial dust, and night's first darkening snow, and the sleep of birds, drift under and through the live dusk of this place of love. Llareggub is the capital of dusk.

Mrs Ogmore-Pritchard, at the first drop of the dusk-shower, seals all her sea-view doors, draws the germ-free blinds, sits, erect as a dry dream on a high-backed hygienic chair and wills herself to cold, quick sleep. At once, at twice, Mr Ogmore and Mr Pritchard, who all dead day long have been gossiping like ghosts in the woodshed, planning the loveless destruction of their glass widow, reluctantly sigh and sidle into her clean house.

MR PRITCHARD

You first, Mr Ogmore.

MR OGMORE

After you, Mr Pritchard.

MR PRITCHARD

No, no, Mr. Ogmore. You widowed her first.

FIRST VOICE

And in through the keyhole, with tears where
their eyes once were, they ooze and grumble.

MRS OGMORE-PRITCHARD

Husbands,

FIRST VOICE

she says in her sleep. There is acid love in her
voice for one of the two shambling phantoms. Mr
Ogmore hopes that it is not for him. So does Mr
Pritchard.

MRS OGMORE-PRITCHARD

I love you both.

MR OGMORE (*With terror*)

Oh, Mrs Ogmore.

MR PRITCHARD (*With horror*)

Oh, Mrs Pritchard.

MRS OGMORE-PRITCHARD

Soon it will be time to go to bed. Tell me your tasks in order.

MR OGMORE AND MR PRITCHARD

We must take our pyjamas from the drawer marked pyjamas.

MRS OGMORE-PRITCHARD (*Coldly*)

And then you must take them off.

SECOND VOICE

Down in the dusking town, Mae Rose Cottage, still lying in clover, listens to the nannygoats chew, draws circles of lipstick round her nipples.

MAE ROSE COTTAGE

I'm *fast*. I'm a bad lot. God will strike me dead. I'm seventeen. I'll go to hell,

SECOND VOICE

she tells the goats.

MAE ROSE COTTAGE

You just wait. I'll sin till I blow up!

SECOND VOICE

She lies deep, waiting for the worst to happen; the goats champ and sneer.

FIRST VOICE

And at the doorway of Bethesda House, the Reverend Jenkins recites to Llareggub Hill his sunset poem.

Every morning when I wake,
Dear Lord, a little prayer I make,
O please to keep Thy lovely eye
On all poor creatures born to die.

And every evening at sun-down
I ask a blessing on the town,
For whether we last the night or no
I'm sure is always touch-and-go.

We are not wholly bad or good
Who live our lives under Milk Wood,
And Thou, I know, wilt be the first
To see our best side, not our worst.

O let us see another day!
Bless us this night, I pray,
And to the sun we all will bow
And say, good-bye—but just for now!

FIRST VOICE

Jack Black prepares once more to meet his Satan
in the Wood. He grinds his night-teeth, closes his
eyes, climbs into his religious trousers, their flies sewn
up with cobbler's thread, and pads out, torched and
bibled, grimly, joyfully, into the already sinning dusk.

JACK BLACK

Off to Gomorrah!

SECOND VOICE

And Lily Smalls is up to Nogood Boyo in the wash-house.

FIRST VOICE

And Cherry Owen, sober as Sunday as he is every day of the week, goes off happy as Saturday to get drunk as a deacon as he does every night.

CHERRY OWEN

I always say she's got two husbands,

FIRST VOICE

says Cherry Owen,

CHERRY OWEN

one drunk and one sober.

FIRST VOICE

And Mrs Cherry simply says

MRS CHERRY OWEN

And aren't I a lucky woman? Because I love them both.

SINBAD

Evening, Cherry.

CHERRY OWEN

Evening, Sinbad.

SINBAD

What'll you have?

88

CHERRY OWEN

Too much.

SINBAD

The Sailors Arms is always open . . .

FIRST VOICE

Sinbad suffers to himself, heartbroken,

SINBAD

. . . oh, Gossamer, open yours!

FIRST VOICE

Dusk is drowned for ever until to-morrow. It is all at once night now. The windy town is a hill of windows, and from the larrupped waves the lights of the lamps in the windows call back the day and the dead that have run away to sea. All over the calling dark, babies and old men are bribed and lullabied to sleep.

FIRST WOMAN'S VOICE

Hushabye, baby, the sandman is coming . . .

SECOND WOMAN'S VOICE (*Singing*)
Rockabye, grandpa, in the tree top,
When the wind blows the cradle will rock,
When the bough breaks the cradle will fall,
Down will come grandpa, whiskers and all.

FIRST VOICE

Or their daughters cover up the old unwinking men like parrots, and in their little dark in the lit and bustling young kitchen corners, all night long they watch, beady-eyed, the long night through in case death catches them asleep.

SECOND VOICE

Unmarried girls, alone in their privately bridal bedrooms, powder and curl for the Dance of the World.

[Accordion music: dim

They make, in front of their looking-glasses, haughty or come-hithering faces for the young men in the street outside, at the lamplit leaning corners, who wait in the all-at-once wind to wolve and whistle.

[Accordion music louder, then fading under

FIRST VOICE

The drinkers in the Sailors Arms drink to the failure of the dance.

A DRINKER

Down with the waltzing and the skipping.

CHERRY OWEN

Dancing isn't natural,

FIRST VOICE

righteously says Cherry Owen who has just downed seventeen pints of flat, warm, thin, Welsh, bitter beer.

SECOND VOICE

A farmer's lantern glimmers, a spark on Llareggub hillside.

[Accordion music fades into silence

Llareggub Hill, writes the Reverend Jenkins in his poem-room,

REVEREND ELI JENKINS

Llareggub Hill, that mystic tumulus, the memorial of peoples that dwelt in the region of Llareggub before the Celts left the Land of Summer and where the old wizards made themselves a wife out of flowers.

SECOND VOICE

Mr Waldo, in his corner of the Sailors Arms, sings:

MR WALDO

In Pembroke City when I was young
I lived by the Castle Keep
Sixpence a week was my wages
For working for the chimbley sweep.
Six cold pennies he gave me
Not a farthing more or less
And all the fare I could afford
Was parsnip gin and watercress.
I did not need a knife and fork
Or a bib up to my chin
To dine on a dish of watercress
And a jug of parsnip gin.
Did you ever hear a growing boy
To live so cruel cheap
On grub that has no flesh and bones
And liquor that makes you weep?
Sweep sweep chimbley sweep,

I wept through Pembroke City
Poor and barefoot in the snow
Till a kind young woman took pity.
Poor little chimbley sweep she said
Black as the ace of spades
O nobody's swept my chimbley
Since my husband went his ways.
Come and sweep my chimbley
Come and sweep my chimbley
She sighed to me with a blush
Come and sweep my chimbley
Come and sweep my chimbley
Bring along your chimbley brush!

FIRST VOICE
Blind Captain Cat climbs into his bunk. Like a cat, he sees in the dark. Through the voyages of his tears, he sails to see the dead.

CAPTAIN CAT
Dancing Williams!

FIRST DROWNED
Still dancing.

CAPTAIN CAT
Jonah Jarvis

THIRD DROWNED
Still.

FIRST DROWNED
Curly Bevan's skull.

ROSIE PROBERT
Rosie, with God. She has forgotten dying.

FIRST VOICE
The dead come out in their Sunday best.

SECOND VOICE
Listen to the night breaking.

FIRST VOICE
Organ Morgan goes to chapel to play the organ.
He sees Bach lying on a tombstone.

ORGAN MORGAN
Johann Sebastian!

CHERRY OWEN (*Drunkenly*)
Who?

ORGAN MORGAN
Johann Sebastian mighty Bach. Oh, Bachfach.

CHERRY OWEN
To hell with you,

FIRST VOICE
says Cherry Owen who is resting on the tomb-
stone on his way home.

Mr Mog Edwards and Miss Myfanwy Price hap-
pily apart from one another at the top and the sea end
of the town write their everynight letters of love and
desire. In the warm White Book of Llareggub you

will find the little maps of the islands of their contentment.

MYFANWY PRICE

Oh, my Mog, I am yours for ever.

FIRST VOICE

And she looks around with pleasure at her own neat neverdull room which Mr Mog Edwards will never enter.

MOG EDWARDS

Come to my arms, Myfanwy.

FIRST VOICE

And he hugs his lovely money to his *own* heart.

And Mr. Waldo drunk in the dusky wood hugs his lovely Polly Garter under the eyes and rattling tongues of the neighbours and the birds, and he does not care. He smacks his live red lips.

But it is not *his* name that Polly Garter whispers as she lies under the oak and loves him back. Six feet deep that name sings in the cold earth.

POLLY GARTER (*Sings*)

But I always think as we tumble into bed
Of little Willy Wee who is dead, dead, dead.

FIRST VOICE

The thin night darkens. A breeze from the creased water sighs the streets close under Milk waking Wood. The Wood, whose every tree-foot's cloven in the black glad sight of the hunters of lovers, that is a God-built

94

garden to Mary Ann Sailors, who knows there is Heaven on earth and the chosen people of His kind fire in Llareggub's land, that is the fairday farmhands' wantoning ignorant chapel of bridesbeds, and, to the Reverend Eli Jenkins, a greenleaved sermon on the innocence of men, the suddenly wind-shaken wood springs awake for the second dark time this one Spring day.

NOTES ON PRONUNCIATION

page 2: *Rhiannon*: strongly aspirated *r*, and accent on the second syllable. *Llareggub*: a voiceless *l* produced from the side of the mouth, accent on the second syllable, the third syllable rhyming with 'bib.' *Dai*: as 'dye.'

page 6: *Dowlais*: accent on the first syllable, the second syllable rhyming with 'ice.' *Maesgwyn*: mice-gwin, accent on the second syllable.

page 7: *Myfanwy*: accent on the second syllable, *f* as *v*, the first *y* an indeterminate sound, the second *y* as *ee*.

page 8: *Ach y fi*: the *ch* guttural, the *y* indeterminate, *f* as *v*, the whole pronounced as one word; an interjection expressing disgust.

page 13: *mwchins*: a compromise between the English 'mooching' and the Welsh dialect word 'mitching,' playing truant.

page 22: *Organ Morgan*: the *r*'s rolled, the *o*'s short. *Gippo*: gipsy.

page 23: *Eisteddfodau*: eye-steth-vod-eye, the *th* voiced, a strong accent on the third syllable. *Parchs*: the *ch* guttural; clergymen.

page 26: *Dewi*: de-wee; the first syllable, which has the accent, is short.

page 27: *Moel yr Wyddfa*: moil-er-ooithva, the *th* voiced. *Carnedd*: the *dd* a voiced *th*, the *r* rolled, accent on the first syllable. *Penmaen-mawr*: 'maen' rhymes with 'line,' 'mawr' with 'hour.'

page 28: *Sawddwy*: southay, the *th* voiced. *Edw*: aid-oo. *Llyfnant*: *y* indeterminate, *f* as *v*. *Claerwen, Cleddau, Dulais*: clire-wen; cleth-eye, the *th* voiced; dill-ice. *Ogwr*: ogoorr, accent on the first syllable. *Cennen*: the *c* hard.

page 42: *Gerwain*: gerr-wine, the *g* hard. *Ty*: as 'tee.'

page 45: *Gorslas*: gorse-lahss, with a strong accent on the second syllable.

page 54: *Twll*: tooll, the *oo* short, the *ll* as in 'Llareg-gub.'

page 66: *cawl*: as 'cowl'; a broth with leeks.

page 93: *fach*: an expression of endearment; *f* as *v*, and the *ch* guttural.

MUSIC FOR THE SONGS

100

Moderate speed (= Tempo I°.)

GIRLS:—
Gwennie call the boys they make such a noise..... *f* Boys boys

GWENNE:—
Boys Come along to me *f* Boys Boys Boys kiss Gwennie where she
GIRLS:—

says or give her a penny GIRLS SPEAK:— Go on, Gwennie.

GWENNE:—
(slow)
p kiss me.... in Goose-gog Lane..... or give me a Tempo I°
f

penny GWENNIE SPEAKS:— What's your name? FIRST BOY SPEAKS:— Billy.

(slow)
GWENNE:—
p kiss... me.... in Goose-gog Lane Billy...... *f* or Tempo I°

give me a pen—ny silly.... *p* Gwennie Gwennie.... I 1st BOY:—(slow)

kiss you in Goose-gog Lane.... (kiss) *f* Now I hasn't got to give you a Tempo I° x (Kiss)

penny... *f* Boys Boys Boys kiss Gwennie where she says or GIRLS:— (Tempo I°.)

give her a penny GIRLS SPEAK:— Go on, Gwennie.

(slow)
GWENNE:—
p Kiss... me.... On Lla— reg—gub Hill.... Or give me a Tempo I°

penny GWENNIE SPEAKS:— What's your name? SECOND BOY SPEAKS:— Johnnie Crisis.

104

In Pembroke City when I was young I lived by the Castle Keep Sixpence a week was my wages For working for the chimbley sweep Six cold pennies he gave me Not a farthing more or less— And all the fare I— could afford was parsnip gin— and watercress I did not need a knife and fork or a bib up to my chin— To dine on a dish of watercress And a jug of parsnip gin. Did you ever hear a growing boy To live so cruel cheap On grub that has no— flesh and bones and liquor that makes you weep? Sweep Sweep chimbley sweep I wept through Pembroke City Poor—and barefoot in the snow   Till a kind young woman took pi—ty —

Poor little chi—mbley sweep she said — Black as the ace of

spades Oh no—body's swept my chi—mbley since my

husband went — his ways   Come—and sweep my

chim—bley   Come—and sweep my chim—bley she

sighed to —me with a blush   Come—and sweep my

chim—bley   Come and sweep my chim—bley Bring a—

—long your chim—bley brush—

107

Complete descriptive catalog available free on request from
New Directions, 333 Sixth Avenue, New York 10014.
† Bilingual.